Edison ES

Many Cultures, One World

# Ethiopia

by Suzanne Delzio

Consultant:
Azeb Tadesse
University of California, Los Angeles
James S. Coleman African Studies Center
Los Angeles, California

Blue Earth Books

an imprint of Capstone Press
Mankato, Minnesota

Blue Earth Books are published by Capstone Press
151 Good Counsel Drive, P.O. Box 669, Mankato, Minnesota 56002
*http://www.capstonepress.com*

*Library of Congress Cataloging-in-Publication Data*
Delzio, Suzanne, 1964–
    Ethiopia / by Suzanne Delzio.
    p. cm.—(Many cultures, one world)
    Summary: An introduction to the geography, history, economy, culture, and people of Ethiopia. Includes a map, legend,
recipe, craft, and game.
    Includes bibliographical references and index.
    ISBN 0-7368-2449-9 (hardcover)
    1. Ethiopia—Juvenile literature. [1. Ethiopia.] I. Title. II. Series.
DT373.D45 2004
963—dc22                                                                         2003012751

**Editorial credits**
Editor: Megan Schoeneberger
Series Designer: Kia Adams
Photo Researcher: Alta Schaffer
Product Planning Editor: Eric Kudalis

**Cover photo**
Blue Nile Falls by Michele Burgess

**Artistic effects**
Rubberball

**Photo credits**
Aurora/Robert Caputo, 14, 18–19, 20
Bob Reis, 23 (bottom right)
Bruce Coleman Inc./Joy Spurr, 16; Norman O. Tomalin, 19 (right)
Capstone Press/Gary Sundermeyer, 3 (all), 21, 25, back cover
Corbis/Gallo Images, 26–27; Lawrence Manning, 9 (right); Rob
    Howard, 4–5
Corbis Sygma/Robert Patrick, 8–9
Cory Langley, 13 (right)
Getty Images Inc./AFP, 22–23; Per-Anders Pettersson, 17
Image Ideas/David van Smeerdijk, 27 (right)
Michele Burgess, 24
One Mile Up Inc., 23 (top right)
Photo Researchers/John Reader, 29 (right)
PictureQuest/Creatas, 11
TRIP/G. Spenceley, 28–29
Victor Englebert, 6, 10, 12–13

1 2 3 4 5 6 09 08 07 06 05 04

# Contents

Turn to page 7 to find a map of Ethiopia.

Check out page 15 to learn to play an Ethiopian game.

Look on page 21 to learn an Ethiopian recipe.

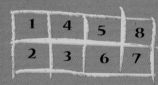

See page 25 to learn to make a lucky charm.

# CHAPTER 1

# Welcome to Ethiopia

Even the best climbers need more than a week to reach the top of Ras Dashen. This mountain is Ethiopia's highest mountain. They climb over sharp rocks and steep cliffs. At the top, they see Ethiopia's countryside below them.

Ethiopia has many high areas. It has more tall mountains than any other African country. High, flat areas called **plateaus** rise near the mountains. Ethiopia's mountains and plateaus are called the highlands. The highlands make up most of Ethiopia.

Mountains stretch across the horizon in Ethiopia. The country's many high areas have given it the nickname "Roof of Africa."

# Facts about Ethiopia

Name: ................Federal Democratic Republic
                    of Ethiopia
Capital: ..............Addis Ababa
Population: .........67 million people
Size: ...................435,184 square miles
                    (1,127,127 square kilometers)
Language: .........Amharic
Religions: ...........Islamic (50 percent), Ethiopian
                    Orthodox (40 percent), other
                    (10 percent)
Highest point: ....Ras Dashen, 15,158 feet
                    (4,620 meters) above sea level
Lowest point: .....Denakil Depression, 410 feet
                    (125 meters) below sea level
Main crops: ........Coffee, oilseed, cereals,
                    potatoes, sugarcane
Money: ..............Birr

5

The rest of Ethiopia is mostly dry. Fields of rock, sand, and dried mud stretch out in all directions. Small trees and grasses grow in the cracked soil.

Ethiopia is a country in a part of northeastern Africa called the Horn of Africa. Eritrea, Djibouti, and Somalia lie north and east of Ethiopia. Together, the countries make the shape of a rhino horn. Kenya lies to Ethiopia's south. Sudan borders Ethiopia to the west. Ethiopia is a little smaller than the U.S. state of Alaska.

The area near Ethiopia's lowest point, the Denakil Depression, is dry and dusty.

# Map of Ethiopia

Red Sea

ERITREA

*Denakil Depression*

◆ Ras Dashen

● Gonder

● Lalibela

SUDAN

● Bahir Dar

DJIBOUTI

*Gulf of Aden*

● Dire Dawa

● Harer

SOMALIA

☆ Addis Ababa

# ETHIOPIA

### Legend
☆ Capital City
● City
◆ Highest Point
∿ Lowest Point
⛰ Mountain

KENYA

*INDIAN OCEAN*

# CHAPTER 2

# An Ethiopian Legend

Ethiopians use legends to teach their children. When the children grow up, they tell these legends to their children. Those children tell their children.

Some Ethiopian legends show what happens when two people argue. In many villages, they go to an elder to settle the argument. An elder is like a judge. The villagers try to pick a fair and smart judge. In one Ethiopian legend, a man and a snake argue. They go to three others for help.

Ethiopians pass stories and legends down to their children. This man is writing in a book made from goatskin.

Ethiopians pass stories from
one generation to the next.

# The Judgment of the Wind

One day, a huge snake slithered into a field where a man was working. The frightened man dropped his tools. He began to run away.

The snake said, "Brother, hide me so the farmers cannot kill me!"

The man stopped running. He knew the angry farmers. They wanted to kill the snake. Earlier that day, the snake had eaten goats and sheep from the farmers' fields.

The man felt sorry for the snake. He told the snake to hide under the cotton. The farmers ran past. They did not see the hidden snake.

After the farmers passed, the snake suddenly took the man's arm in his mouth. The man twisted to get free, but the snake was strong.

"I just saved your life," the man said. "Why do you wish to eat me?"

"I am hungry!" the snake said.

An Ethiopian farmer uses oxen to help plow his fields.

The snake and the man argued. They decided to ask the tree, the grass, and the wind what they should do.

The man told the tree what happened. The tree said, "Man breaks my branches. Man is not good. It is right that the snake eats the man."

The man told the grass what happened. The grass said, "Man rips me from the ground to make baskets. Man is not good. It is right that the snake eats the man."

"This judgment is not fair!" the man said. The two walked farther. They met the wind. The man told his story.

The wind said, "The tree needs its branches to live. The grass grows to live. The snake eats man to live. One cannot blame the tree, the grass, or the snake. They all do what they must."

The wind gave the snake and the man drums to play. To hold its drum, the snake had to let go of the man. The wind sang to the snake. "As you want to eat man, eat man." The wind turned to the farmer. "As you do not want to be eaten, do not be eaten!"

The man listened to the wind and ran safely to his village.

Green mamba snakes hide easily in green plants and trees in southern Ethiopia. The deadly snake can swallow objects four times larger than its head.

# CHAPTER 3

# City and Country Life

Ethiopia is a beautiful but poor country. Most families live on small farms in the highlands. They grow food and raise farm animals. They do not own tractors or trucks. Instead, they use oxen to pull wooden plows through the thick soil.

Ethiopians who live in the desert are called **nomads**. They do not settle in any one place. They travel and make camp where they find water. They build, take down, and carry their huts. The nomads build their huts again when they find a place to stop.

Nomad families build huts that are easy to build, take down, and carry. They move often in search of food and water in the desert.

In the highlands, families herd goats and raise other farm animals.

Few Ethiopians live in cities. Dire Dawa, Gonder, Harer, and Bahir Dar are small cities. Ethiopia's capital and largest city, Addis Ababa, is in the center of the country. More than five million people live there.

Many people who live in Addis Ababa are very poor. They build their homes from mud and grass. These homes do not have electricity or running water.

The people who work in government or business in Addis Ababa earn more money. They live in apartment buildings or large houses with refrigerators, ovens, and TVs. They may work in high-rise office buildings.

Addis Ababa is one of the few large cities in Ethiopia.

# Mancha

Children in Ethiopia often play *mancha*. *Mancha* is like hopscotch. As players get better at it, they make it harder. For example, players may have to throw the stone with their eyes closed. Players can also stop other players from entering certain spaces.

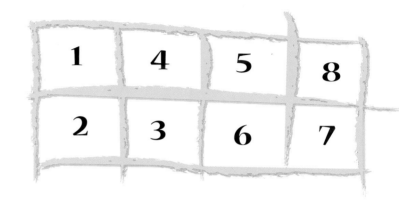

## What You Need

a sidewalk
two or more players
a stone for each player
a piece of chalk

## What You Do

1. With chalk, draw a grid as shown in the picture. Write numbers inside each square.
2. Throw a stone into the first square.
3. Hop on one foot into the first square. As you jump, kick the stone into the second square using only the foot you are hopping on. Do not let the other foot touch the ground.
4. If the stone lands in the second square, hop and kick the stone again into the next square.
5. Keep going until you have kicked the stone into all eight squares in order.
6. If the stone lands outside of the correct space or touches a line, pick it up. Another player gets a turn. You are out until that player's stone lands outside a square or on a line. Then you must start over at the beginning.
7. The first player to move through all eight squares wins the game.

# CHAPTER 4

# Seasons in Ethiopia

In September, green plants and yellow flowers cover the hills and mountains of Ethiopia.

In Ethiopia, temperatures do not change much throughout the year. People wear the same type of clothes in December that they wear in August.

The amount of rainfall marks the end of one season and the start of another. Light rains begin during March in the highlands. The ground becomes soft. In most areas, a large amount of rain falls during June, July, and August. Snow covers the tops of high mountains. By early September, the rains stop. Flowers bloom, and trees turn green.

Some years, enough rain falls in winter. Other years, no rain falls at all. Without rain, food cannot grow. The people and their animals have nothing to eat. Times without enough food are called **famines**. Ethiopia has had many famines.

When there is not enough rain, the land becomes dry. People look for fresh water and carry it in jugs back to their villages.

17

# CHAPTER 5

# Family Life in Ethiopia

Ethiopian families are often large. Most families have about seven children. The children help with the housework.

Farming in the highlands is a big job. The children help their parents. When monkeys and birds come into fields, children chase them away. Children also find wood for cooking. While parents work, older children care for their younger brothers and sisters.

Children stand on platforms to watch for monkeys and birds. They scare the animals away from the fields.

# Gelada Baboons

Ethiopian children often chase gelada baboons (JEH-luh-duh ba-BOONS) out of their families' crops. The gelada baboon is a medium-sized monkey. It has a long snout, big teeth, and a long tail. These baboons try to eat the roots of plants growing in farmers' fields.

Parents often wait a few weeks to name their children. They wait to see what the child will be like. They often give children hopeful names. For example, Allefnew means "we made it through the bad times." The name Tesfaye means "my hope."

Most Ethiopians do not celebrate birthdays. Families often do not have enough money for gifts, games, or food. Children who live in cities sometimes have birthday parties with special food and gifts. One group of Ethiopians, the Oromo, celebrates a child's growth every eight years.

Ethiopian parents often wait to see their baby's personality before choosing a name.

# Dabo Kolo

*Dabo kolo* means "little fried snacks." These crunchy treats can be served before a meal, as a snack, or as a dessert. Be sure to ask an adult for help or permission to use the stove.

## What You Need

### Ingredients
2 cups (480 mL) flour
½ teaspoon (2.5 mL) salt
2 tablespoons (30 mL) sugar
¾ teaspoon (2.5 mL) cayenne pepper
¾ cup (175 mL) water
extra flour (for cutting surface)
¼ cup (60 mL) oil

### Equipment
dry-ingredient measuring cups
measuring spoons
liquid measuring cup
1-quart (1-liter) bowl
mixing spoon
cutting surface
rolling pin
knife
frying pan
spatula

## What You Do

1. Measure all ingredients except oil and extra flour into a bowl.
2. Stir with a mixing spoon until dry ingredients are moistened. If needed, add 1 to 3 tablespoons (15 mL to 45 mL) of water to the dough.
3. Sprinkle extra flour over a cutting surface.
4. Roll dough over the floured cutting surface, kneading the dough until it is smooth.
5. With a rolling pin, roll the dough to about ½ inch (1 centimeter) thick.
6. Use a knife to cut the dough into 1-inch (2-centimeter) squares.
7. Cover the bottom of a frying pan with oil. Add the dough squares.
8. Cook over medium heat, using a spatula to turn pieces as they cook, until pieces are light brown on both sides.

Makes about 4 dozen 1-inch (2-centimeter) squares

*CHAPTER 6*

# Laws, Rules, and Customs

A **democracy** rules Ethiopia. The people choose the country's president and **prime minister**. They also choose other leaders from different parts of the country. These leaders help the prime minister make laws.

Ethiopia's prime minister has the same role as the U.S. president. He leads the government. He is in charge of Ethiopia's army.

In Ethiopia, men and women vote for the president and the prime minister.

A blue circle with a yellow star sits in the center of Ethiopia's flag. The flag has one green, one yellow, and one red stripe. The green stripe stands for the country's farms. The yellow stripe stands for religious freedom. The red stripe honors the people who fought to bring better government to Ethiopia.

Ethiopian money is called birr. In the early 2000s, about 8 Ethiopian birr equaled one U.S. dollar.

Ethiopia also has a president. The president does not do the same job as the prime minister. He gives out awards and attends ceremonies.

More than half of Ethiopian children go to school. A child often shares the classroom with up to 40 other children. Students take turns using books.

On March 2 of every year, Ethiopians celebrate Victory of Adwa Day. The holiday marks the day in 1896 when Ethiopia won a battle against Italy. People march in parades. They sing about their loyalty to their country. Ethiopians wear their finest white clothing.

Ethiopian children often share the classroom with many other children.

# Make a Lucky Charm

Many of the Oromo people of Ethiopia wear special charms. They hope the charms will help good things come to them and keep bad things away. You can make your own lucky charms.

## What You Need

oven-bake clay
bamboo skewer
cord
pony beads (if desired)

## What You Do

1. Take a piece of clay about the size of a marble.
2. Work the clay by rubbing it between the palms of your hands until it becomes soft.
3. Shape the clay into a rectangular shape.
4. Use a bamboo skewer to make a hole near the top of the clay charm. Gently wiggle the skewer around to make sure the hole is big enough for the cord to go through.
5. Use the point of the bamboo skewer to make small holes on the surfaces of the charm.
6. Repeat steps 1 through 5 to make more rectangular clay charms.
7. Bake clay according to package directions.
8. Thread the cord with the clay charms, putting a pony bead between each one. Tie the two ends of the string together and wear the charms around your neck.

# CHAPTER 7

# Pets in Ethiopia

Many Ethiopian families do not have pets. Those families who do have pets usually own dogs or cats. Some families raise birds called **doves**.

In the country, Ethiopian families take good care of their oxen, goats, and sheep. They treat the animals like pets. Children train dogs to protect the farm animals.

Ethiopians build indoor pens for mules, cows, sheep, and other animals. Some homes even have a pen for horses. Farm animals are safer indoors. Hungry wild dogs and hyenas hunt at night.

Older children sometimes tend cattle and other livestock.

# Ethiopian Animals

Ethiopia has many wild animals. Herds of zebras and **gazelles** race across the land. In the grasslands, Ethiopians stay away from elephants, cheetahs, and lions. Children playing near lakes and rivers sometimes see hippos or alligators.

One-third of the world's frog species live only in Ethiopia. Several frogs have developed special, even strange, ways to live. Two kinds of Ethiopian frogs swallow snails whole. They eat both the snail and its shell.

# CHAPTER 8

# Sights to See in Ethiopia

Ethiopia's historical and natural riches attract visitors. In the small town of Lalibela, 800-year-old churches carved from solid rock rise from the ground. Inside, tunnels connect underground rooms. It may have taken 40,000 workers to carve the churches.

The *Merkato* in Addis Ababa offers many goods. Thousands of people come to this huge open market. Buyers find row after row of items for sale. People argue for the best price. Friends who have not seen each other for a while meet again. Laughter comes from all directions.

This church in Lalibela is carved from solid rock.

# Lucy

Some scholars believe the human race began in Ethiopia. In 1974, people found a small skeleton in northeast Ethiopia. It looked like a monkey. Still, it had a jaw, teeth, and hips just like a human. Tests found that it was a 3-million-year-old female human. They named her Lucy. Lucy is the oldest human skeleton. People can see Lucy in Addis Ababa's National Museum.

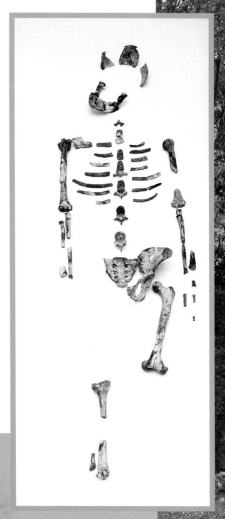

# Glossary

**democracy** (de-MOK-ruh-see)—a type of government where people vote for their leaders

**dove** (DUHV)—a bird that makes a gentle cooing sound

**famine** (FAM-uhn)—a serious shortage of food resulting in widespread hunger and death

**gazelle** (guh-ZEL)—a graceful antelope found in Africa and Asia; gazelles can run very fast.

**nomad** (NOH-mad)—a person who moves to find food and water, rather than living in one place

**plateau** (pla-TOH)—an area of high, flat land

**prime minister** (PRIME MIN-uh-stur)—the person in charge of the government of some countries; Ethiopia has a prime minister who leads the government.

# Read More

**Berg, Elizabeth.** *Ethiopia.* Festivals of the World. Milwaukee: Gareth Stevens, 1999.

**Britton, Tamara L.** *Ethiopia.* The Countries. Edina, Minn.: Abdo, 2002.

**Lassieur, Allison.** *Ethiopia.* Countries and Cultures. Mankato, Minn.: Capstone Press, 2003.

**Schemenauer, Elma.** *Ethiopia.* Faces and Places. Chanhassen, Minn.: Child's World, 2001.

# Useful Addresses

**Embassy of Ethiopia—Canada**
#210-151 Slater Street
Ottawa, Ontario  K1P 5H3
Canada

**Embassy of Ethiopia—United States**
3506 International Drive NW
Washington, DC  20008

**Horn of Africa Services**
4714 Rainier Avenue South, Suite 105
Seattle, WA  98118

**UCLA James S. Coleman African Studies Center**
405 Hilgard Avenue
10244 Bunche Hall
Los Angeles, CA  90095

# Internet Sites

FactHound offers a safe, fun way to find Internet sites related to this book.
All of the sites on FactHound have been researched by our staff.

### Here's how:

1. Visit *www.facthound.com*
2. Type in this special code **0736824499** for age-appropriate sites. Or enter a search word related to this book for a more general search.
3. Click on the **Fetch It** button.

**FactHound will fetch the best sites for you!**

# Index